A DK PUBLISHING BOOK

Editor Julie Ferris
Art editor Diane Clouting
Managing editor Gill Denton
Managing art editor Julia Harris
Production Charlotte Traill
Picture research Mollie Gillard
DTP designer Nicola Studdart
Illustrators Eric Thomas, Amy Burch

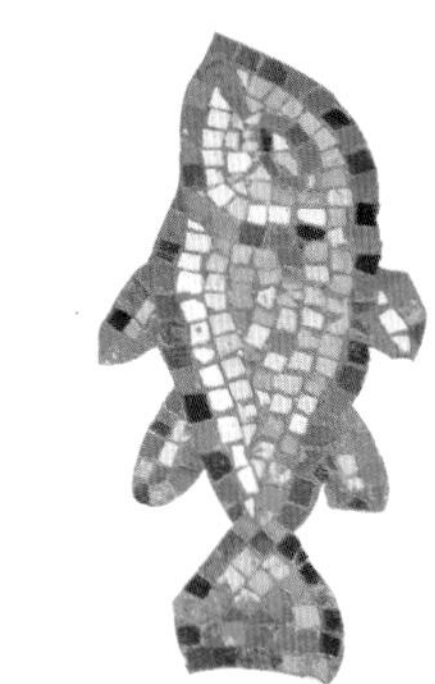

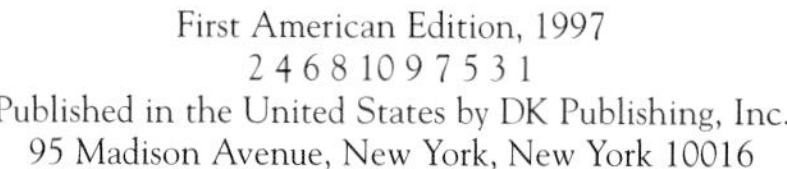

First American Edition, 1997
2 4 6 8 10 9 7 5 3 1
Published in the United States by DK Publishing, Inc.
95 Madison Avenue, New York, New York 10016

Visit us on the World Wide Web at http://www.dk.com

Published in Great Britain by Dorling Kindersley Ltd.

A CIP catalog record for this book is available from the Library of Congress.

ISBN 0-7894-1899-1

Color reproduction by Colourscan, Singapore
Printed and bound in Belgium by Proost

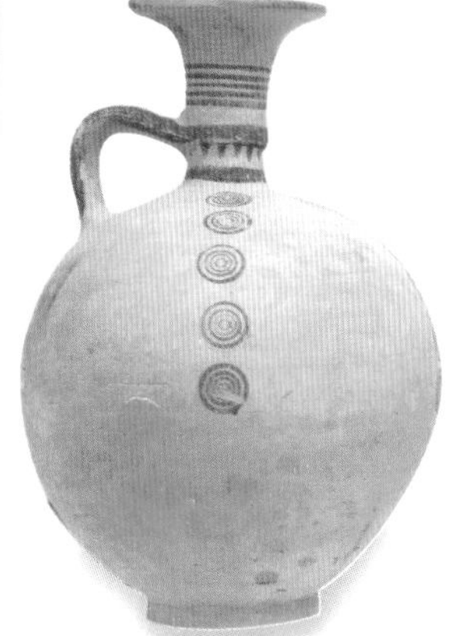

BIBLE QUESTIONS & ANSWERS

by David Pickering

The Holy Book

The Bible is the best-selling book in the world. People all around the world respect it as the "Word of God," a book inspired by God, although written by human authors. It is divided into two parts. The Old Testament is the Jewish Bible, the New Testament was written by Christians. Both Old and New Testaments are made up of a number of small books collected together.

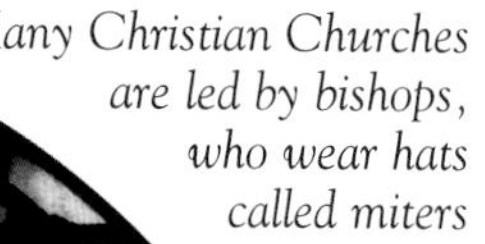

Many Christian Churches are led by bishops, who wear hats called miters

People find spiritual strength through reading the Bible and prayer

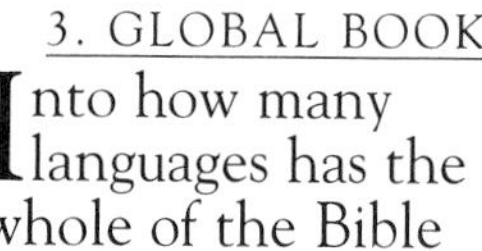

Stained-glass windows often depict Bible stories

1. THE BIBLE

What does "Bible" mean?

- Word of God
- books
- wise oracle

2. ONE GOD

In Old Testament times, when other nations had many temples and many gods, the Jewish people had one God and one Temple. Where was this temple?

- Babylon
- Jerusalem
- Rome

There was a seven-branched candle similar to this Hanukkah candle in the Old Testament Temple

3. GLOBAL BOOK

Into how many languages has the whole of the Bible been translated?

- 249
- 349
- 449

4. NEW LANGUAGE

The Old Testament was written in Hebrew. What language was the New Testament written in?

- Greek
- Latin
- Aramaic

5. ANIMALS

Animals appear in many Bible stories. Which animal is mentioned most often in the Bible?

- the serpent
- the sheep
- the lion

6. LEADER

Did Jesus say that He wanted a leader in the Church to be:

- the cleverest of all
- the hardest working of all
- the servant of all?

Christians together make up the "Church," so the buildings they meet in are called churches

7. BIBLE SETTING

Most of the events in the Bible take place in Palestine, a small land in the Middle East, most of which is now part of the state of Israel. What was Palestine originally called?

- Edom
- Canaan
- Aram

The cross is the main symbol of Christianity because Jesus died by being nailed to a cross

9. OLDEST SCROLLS

The oldest Biblical manuscripts known are about 2,000 years old. Where were they found?

- by the Red Sea
- by the Dead Sea
- by the Sea of Galilee

10. BIBLE WRITERS

How many people wrote the Bible?

- fewer than 10
- between 10 and 30
- more than 30

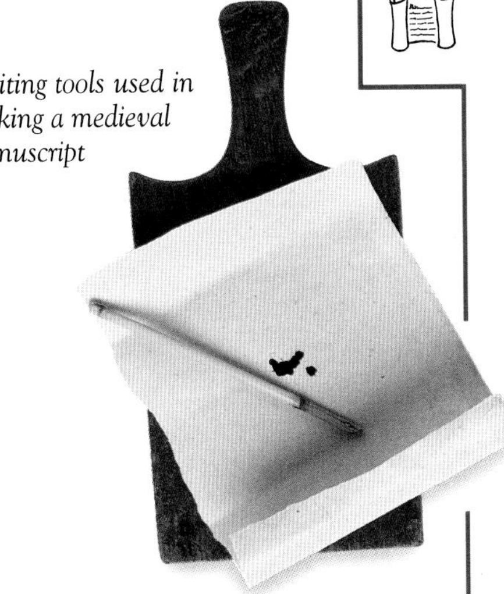

Writing tools used in making a medieval manuscript

12. BIBLE DIVISIONS

The Old Testament books can be divided into four categories: law, history, prophecy, and wisdom books. Which category do the Psalms fall in?

- history
- prophecy
- wisdom books

Medieval manuscripts took many years to complete. They are often beautifully decorated

The Old Testament was written in Hebrew; Jewish people still use Hebrew in their worship

8. THE LAW

The first five books of the Bible, together known as the Pentateuch, contain the Law by which Orthodox Jewish people live. What is this Law called?

- the Torah
- the Mishnah
- the Talmud

The Bible was first printed by Johannes Gutenberg. This is his printing press

11. PRINT

Through the centuries, more copies of the Bible have been produced than of any other book. In what year was the Bible first printed?

- 1355
- 1455
- 1555

In the beginning

Creation was completed in six days. On the seventh day God rested

The first chapters of the Bible tell stories about the beginning of the world and the earliest days of human existence. God created everything good, but Adam and Eve, the first humans, chose to disobey Him and humanity became distant from God. God still cared for human beings, however, and called on a man named Abraham to follow Him and found a nation.

A serpent tempted the first humans to disobey God

1. SIX DAYS

God created the world in six days. What was created on the first day?

- the sun and moon
- day and night
- land and sea

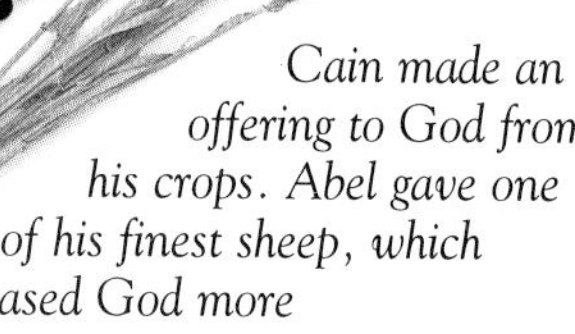

Cain made an offering to God from his crops. Abel gave one of his finest sheep, which pleased God more

2. MURDER

Which of Adam and Eve's sons was the world's first murderer?

- Cain
- Abel
- Seth

3. GREAT FLOOD

God was angry with the wickedness on earth and caused a flood to destroy every living thing. Who did God tell to build an Ark to save his family and two of every creature?

- Joseph
- Noah
- Jonah

Two of every kind of creature were sheltered in the Ark

4. THE TOWER

Early people tried to build a tower that reached the heavens at a place called Babel. Is Babel better known as:

- Bethlehem
- Babylon
- Baghdad?

5. PARADISE

God made a home for Adam and Eve in Eden. Was it:

- a palace
- a garden
- a city?

6. SIGN FROM GOD

Rain continued for forty days and forty nights. At the end of the flood God sent a sign. Was it:

- a pillar of fire
- a white dove
- a rainbow?

Brueghel's painting of the Tower of Babel

7. ABRAHAM'S JOURNEYS

God chose Abram to found His people. He renamed him Abraham, which means "father of many." Where did Abraham come from?

- modern-day Turkey
- modern-day Iraq
- modern-day Iran

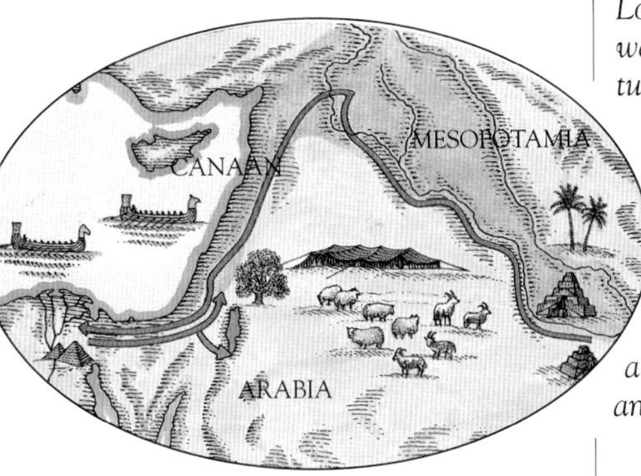

Abraham lived a nomadic lifestyle and traveled widely

8. ANCIENT ANCESTRY

Which two Middle-Eastern peoples can trace their ancestry back to Abraham?

9. GREATEST SACRIFICE

Abraham trusted God so much that he was willing to sacrifice his own son if God wanted him to. Was Abraham's son named:

- Isaac
- Melchizedek
- Moses?

Lentil stew with unleavened bread was a common meal

10. INHERITANCE

Who gave up his inheritance rights as an eldest son for a bowl of stew?

- Lot
- Jacob
- Esau

Lot's wife looked back as the cities were being destroyed and was turned into a pillar of salt

11. NEW NAME

Jacob was the son of Isaac. God renamed him. Did he call him:

- Canaan
- Israel
- Benjamin?

12. PILLAR OF SALT

Abraham's nephew Lot lived in a city by the Dead Sea. This city was famous for the wickedness of its people, and God destroyed it. Was the city called:

- Sodom
- Gomorrah
- Eilat?

Abraham was prepared to sacrifice his son

13. OLD AGE

According to the Book of Genesis, who lived to be the oldest person in the Bible?

- Adam
- Seth
- Methuselah

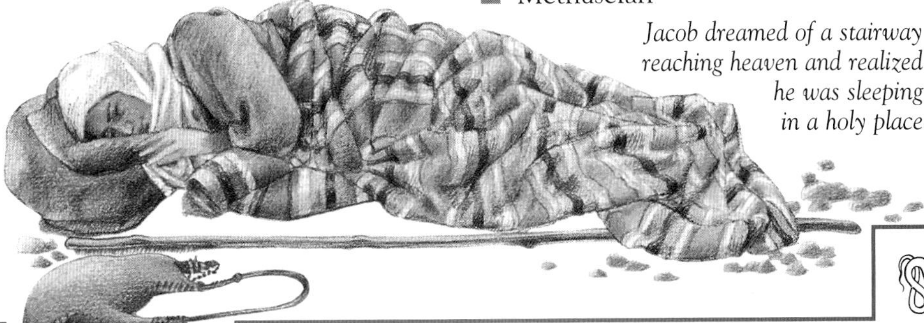

Jacob dreamed of a stairway reaching heaven and realized he was sleeping in a holy place

The Israelites in Egypt

Jacob's son Joseph was taken to Egypt as a slave. He rose to become the king of Egypt's second-in-command by interpreting the ruler's dreams and predicting a terrible famine. Jacob and the rest of his family went to Egypt to join Joseph and to escape famine in their own land. Their descendants stayed there for centuries, and grew into a nation.

Jacob gave Joseph a beautiful coat of many colors, which made his brothers jealous

1. FAVORITE SON

Joseph was Jacob's favorite son. How many sons did Jacob have?

- seven
- ten
- twelve

2. JOSEPH'S DREAM

Joseph had a dream in which he and his brothers were binding sheaves of corn in a field. In his dream, what did his brothers' sheaves of corn do?

Joseph's dream about sheaves of corn foretold the time when he would be powerful in Egypt

Ramses II was ruler of Egypt at the time of Moses

3. SLAVERY

At the time of Moses, the Israelites were forced to work as slaves for the king of Egypt. What was the king of Egypt called?

- emperor
- pharaoh
- sphinx

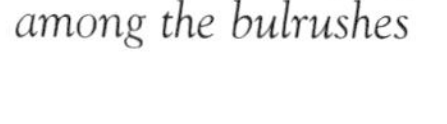

Moses was found in a basket, lying among the bulrushes

4. BIRTH OF MOSES

About 300 years after Joseph's time, the Egyptians enslaved the Israelites. The Israelites were eventually led out of Egypt by Moses, who was brought up by the daughter of the ruler of Egypt. Did she find Moses:

- in his house
- in the river
- on the roof of the palace?

5. GOD'S PLAGUES

When the Israelites wanted to leave Egypt, the king refused to let them go, so God sent plagues to Egypt until the Israelites were released. How many plagues were there?

- five
- seven
- ten

God sent a plague of locusts to Egypt and they ate all the crops

6. PUNISHMENT

When the Israelites first asked to leave Egypt, instead of letting them go, the king punished them by ordering them to make:

- bread without yeast
- boats without wood
- bricks without straw?

The ancient Egyptians treated slaves very harshly

7. EGYPTIAN RELIGION

Religion was important to the ancient Egyptians. How many gods did they worship?

- one
- two
- many

Amulets were worn as good-luck charms

8. TRIBES OF ISRAEL

The tribes of Israel are descended from the sons of Jacob. From which son did the priests' tribe come?

- Joseph
- Simeon
- Levi

9. TO THE PROMISED LAND

Egypt was a rich land, home to many delicious foods. Was the land to which the Israelites journeyed when they left Egypt described as a land of:

- meat and manna
- milk and honey
- lentils and leeks?

Typical native Egyptian food

10. BURNING BUSH

While he was working as a shepherd in the desert, Moses came across a bush that was on fire but did not burn up at all. Who spoke to him from this bush?

- Angel Gabriel
- the devil
- God

11. BROTHER OF MOSES

Moses' brother became the first high priest of Israel. What was his name?

- Judah
- Jesse
- Aaron

Moses receives a message from a burning bush

The Exodus

This meal is eaten at a Jewish festival. Each ingredient has a special meaning

When God delivered His people from slavery in Egypt, they set out toward Canaan, the Promised Land. Led by Moses, they spent many years in the wilderness. The story of their flight from Egypt and their years in the wilderness is called the Exodus.

God called Moses to Him and gave him the Ten Commandments carved on stone tablets

1. FREEDOM

At which special annual meal do Jews remember how God delivered them from Egypt?

- the Last Supper
- the Passover
- Thanksgiving

The Israelites may have carried their possessions in saddle bags similar to this

2. TEN COMMANDMENTS

Where did God give Moses the Ten Commandments by which He wished His people to live?

- Jerusalem
- Mount Sinai
- Mount Everest

God parted the Red Sea so that His people could escape from Pharaoh. He closed it again to drown Pharaoh's army

3. WILDERNESS

God guided the Israelites through the wilderness. By day a pillar of cloud went ahead of them. What guided them at night?

- a pillar of salt
- a pillar of light
- a pillar of fire

While Moses was away, the Israelites made a golden statue to worship

4. FALSE IDOL

The Israelites worshiped a golden statue of which animal?

- a donkey
- a lamb
- a calf

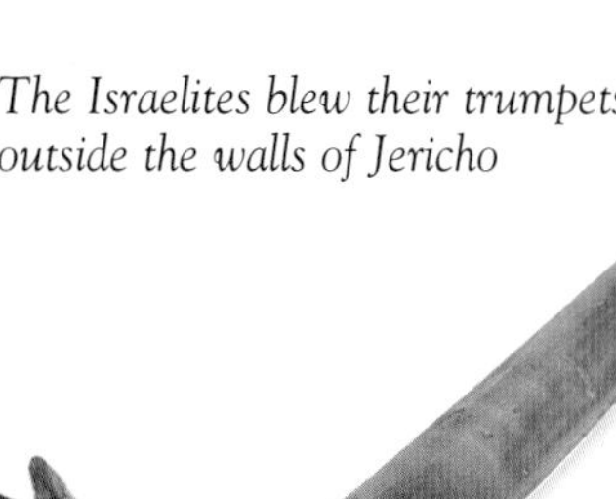

The Israelites blew their trumpets outside the walls of Jericho

5. FORTY YEARS

The Israelites had to spend 40 years in the wilderness because they disobeyed God. God fed them with manna. What food was manna like?

- wafers
- cornflakes
- potatoes

Donkeys appear in many Bible stories

6. TALKING DONKEY

Which Old Testament prophet was told what to do by his donkey?

- Elijah
- Jeremiah
- Balaam

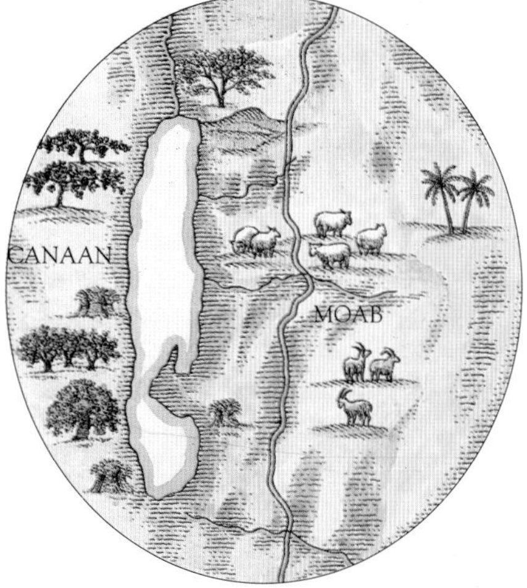

The Promised Land

7. WILDERNESS FOOD

In addition to manna, what else did God send to feed the Israelites in the wilderness?

- quail
- chicken
- duck

8. TRUMPETS

What happened when the Israelites blew their trumpets outside Jericho?

- the gates blew open
- the city was destroyed
- the walls fell down

9. LEADERS

Who led the Israelites after they first settled in the Promised Land?

- kings
- judges
- priests

10. MOSES

Moses led the Israelites for the 40 years of their wanderings in the wilderness. Did he lead them into the Promised Land?

Priests carrying the Ark of the Covenant

11. ARK OF THE COVENANT

The Ark of the Covenant was carried by the Israelites on their journey. What was kept in it?

Food was plentiful in the Promised Land

After 40 years, Moses finally got to see the Promised Land

Prophets and kings

Samson killed a lion with his bare hands

1. STRONG MAN

What was the secret of Samson's great strength?

- his diet
- his hair
- his muscles

2. HOLY MAN

Samuel was a holy priest. God told him who to choose to be the first king of Israel. Who was chosen?

- Herod
- David
- Saul

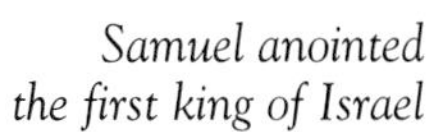

Samuel anointed the first king of Israel

Gradually, the Israelites strayed from God. God sent prophets to His people to call them back to Him, but the Israelites paid little attention. Their kingdom split and they were conquered. Eventually they returned from exile and rebuilt Jerusalem.

Samuel devoted his life to serving God. He was brought up by a priest

3. GIANT SLAYER

Who rose from shepherd boy to king of Israel and killed the giant, Goliath, with his sling?

- David
- Solomon
- Julius Caesar

4. PROVERBS

Which one of the following proverbs is in the Bible?

- a stitch in time saves nine
- all's well that ends well
- a cheerful look brings joy to the heart

5. BEARING GIFTS

From which queen did King Solomon receive great gifts?

- the queen of Egypt
- the queen of Sheba
- the queen of England

A stained-glass window depicting the slaying of Goliath

Goliath was killed by a slingshot and stones

6. WISE LEADER

Which king built the Temple in Jerusalem and was famous for his wisdom?

Solomon received many great gifts

Ravens helped the prophet Elijah in the desert

7. PROPHET IN THE WILDERNESS

Elijah fled into the desert to escape a cruel king. God sent ravens to help him. What did they do?

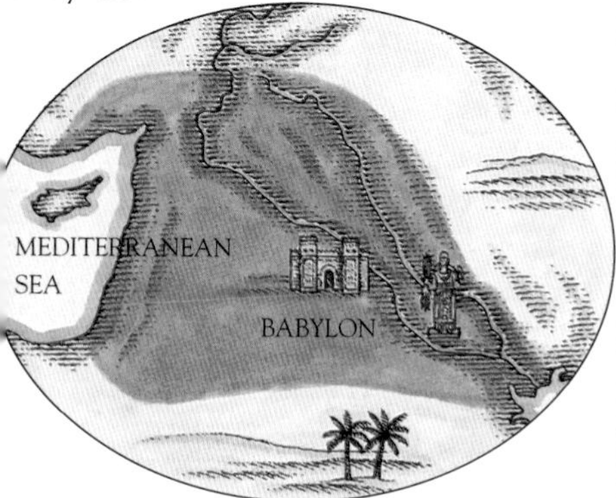

The Babylonian Empire

8. EXILE

After the Israelites turned away from God, they were taken as slaves to Babylon. How long were they in slavery for?

- 50 years
- 70 years
- 90 years

Jews remember the heroic actions of the queen who saved the Israelites from death at an annual festival

9. SAVING HER PEOPLE

Who married the king of Persia and saved her people from death?

- Esther
- Mary
- Marjorie

10. WRITING

Which king of Babylon saw his fate being written on the wall?

- Nebuchadnezzar
- Belshazzar
- Darius

11. PROPHECY

Which prophet foretold a "suffering servant" who would bring peace?

- Jeremiah
- Amos
- Isaiah

12. FISHY TALE

Which prophet was told by God to go to Nineveh, but ran away and was swallowed by a whale?

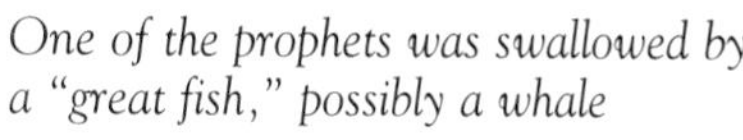

One of the prophets was swallowed by a "great fish," possibly a whale

13. FAITH IN GOD

Why did King Darius throw his favorite servant Daniel to the lions?

Daniel was protected by God and the lions did not harm him

The Israelite slaves were treated harshly by the Babylonians

The birth of Jesus

The town where Jesus was born

God promised the Jewish people that He would send them a special leader, the Messiah, to save them and guide them. Christians believe that Jesus was this leader: the Son of God. The story of His birth is recorded in the New Testament and is called the Nativity story.

Mary was told she would have a child. This event is called the Annunciation

1. HOLY BIRTHPLACE

Jesus grew up in the town of Nazareth. In what town was He born?

- Jerusalem
- Nazareth
- Bethlehem

2. MARY AND JOSEPH

Jesus' mother Mary was married to a man named Joseph. Was Joseph:

- a shepherd
- a carpenter
- a tax collector?

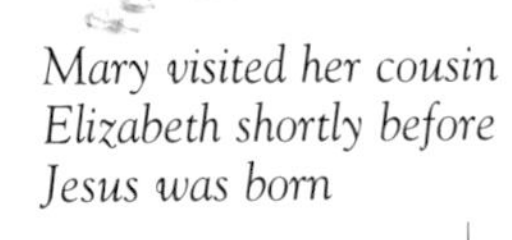

Mary visited her cousin Elizabeth shortly before Jesus was born

5. ANNUNCIATION

According to the Bible, Jesus had God as His father instead of a human father. Who told Jesus' mother, Mary, that she was pregnant?

Shepherds often had to stay out all night watching over their flocks

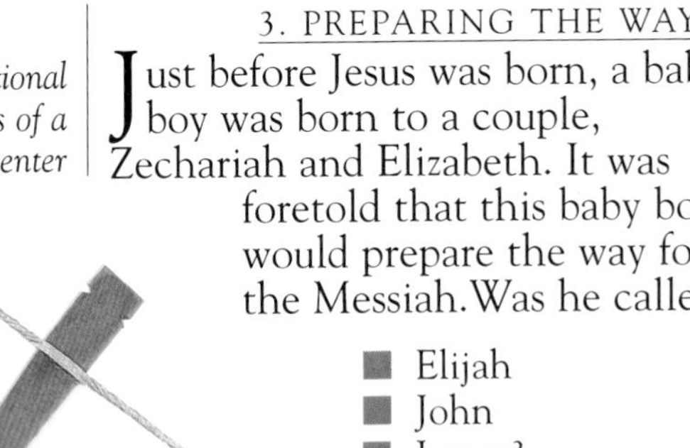

Traditional tools of a carpenter

3. PREPARING THE WAY

Just before Jesus was born, a baby boy was born to a couple, Zechariah and Elizabeth. It was foretold that this baby boy would prepare the way for the Messiah. Was he called:

- Elijah
- John
- James?

4. GOD WITH US

Which name used to describe Jesus means "God with us"?

- Messiah
- Emmanuel
- Christ

6. RULERS

Who ruled the land of Palestine when Jesus was born?

- the Greeks
- the Romans
- the Jews

7. FIRST TO HEAR

Who were the first people to e told that Jesus had een born?

- wise men
- local shepherds
- Bethlehem town council

Angels announced the news that Jesus had been born

8. PRECIOUS GIFTS

After His birth, Jesus was given gold, frankincense, and yrrh. Who gave Him these gifts?

old, frankincense, nd myrrh were precious bjects in the time f Jesus

9. ANGELS

Angels appear in many New Testament stories. What does angel mean?

- "shining one"
- "messenger"
- "sword-bearer"

10. FLEEING HEROD

After Jesus was born, King Herod wanted to kill Him, so Joseph and Mary had to run away. To which country did they go?

- Syria
- Iraq
- Egypt

King Herod ordered every boy under the age of two to be put to death

Jesus was born in a stable and laid in a manger

Stories and miracles

When Jesus was about 30, He began to travel, teaching, healing, and performing miracles (supernatural acts). He gathered around Him a group of disciples (followers).

1. DESERT DIET

Which famous person in the Gospels lived in the desert and ate honey and locusts?

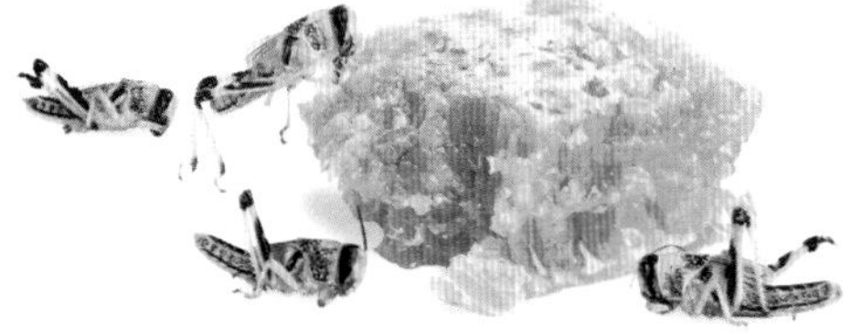

Locusts are eaten in areas where meat is scarce. Honey counteracts their bitter taste

2. BAPTISM

John the Baptist baptized Jesus at the start of His ministry (public work). Where did this baptism take place?

- Jerusalem
- the Sea of Galilee
- the Jordan River

3. THE GOSPELS

The Gospels record Jesus' life and teaching. How many Gospels are there?

- two
- four
- five

4. DISCIPLES

Did Jesus tell His disciples that they would be:

- famous leaders
- holy saints
- fishers of men?

Jesus calls Peter and Andrew to join Him as disciples

Baptism was a ritual cleansing of sins. Today, it is a rite of entry into the Christian Church

5. MINISTRY

Which of the following names did Jesus use to describe Himself?

- Good Shepherd
- Good Carpenter
- Good Fisherman

6. TEMPTATION

Jesus spent forty days and nights in the wilderness. Who tempted Him there?

These vultures live in desert wilderness area like the one in which Jesus spent forty days

7. GOSPEL SAYINGS

Which of these saying is not found in the Gospels:

- Love your enemies
- It is more blessed to give than to receive
- Blessed are the pure in heart?

8. HONEST QUESTION

In the Gospels, only one person came to Jesus with an honest question and left Him sad because of the answer. Who was it?

- Jairus's mother
- a Samaritan woman
- a rich, young ruler

9. RELIGIOUS LEADERS

Jesus spent much time arguing with members of a very strict religious group What was this group called

- the Pharisees
- the Sadducees
- the Essenes

Jesus spent forty days and nights in the wilderness

Wine was a popular drink in Bible times

Five loaves and two fish

10. FEAST

One of Jesus' most famous miracles was feeding many people with five loaves and two fish. How many people were fed?

- 500
- 1,000
- 5,000

11. FRIENDS

Jesus had three friends who lived at Bethany, near Jerusalem, named Mary, Martha, and Lazarus. Which of them did he raise from the dead?

Martha once quarreled with Mary about listening to Jesus rather than helping with the household chores

12. WATER INTO WINE

Where did Jesus perform His first miracle?

- at a wedding
- at a funeral
- in a synagogue

13. TRANSFIGURATION

Jesus explained to His disciples that He would die, and, on the third day after His death, He would rise again. He took three disciples to a mountain to pray and heavenly light shone down as Jesus spoke to:

- Moses and Elijah
- David and Solomon
- Moses and Adam?

Jesus had power to heal the sick

Peter, James, and John witnessed the Transfiguration, when Jesus spoke to two prophets

Teaching and traveling

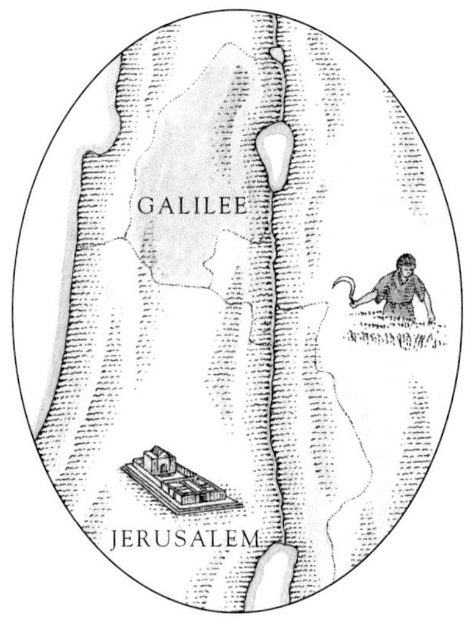

Jesus and His disciples traveled widely

As Jesus traveled around the country, many came to hear Him teach, but some of the religious leaders were against Him. He often taught in parables, simple stories in which everyday things and ordinary people are used to illustrate spiritual truths and moral behavior.

A sower's ba

1. DISCIPLES

A group of twelve of Jesus' disciples were particularly close to Him and traveled with Him all the time. What were they known as?

3. WRITTEN RECORD

Is there any record of Jesus writing down any of His teachings himself?

- yes
- no
- a few things

5. WORD OF GOD

One parable is about seeds being scattered on different kinds of soil. The seeds represent the Word of God. What is the parable called

- parable of the preacher
- parable of the seed
- parable of the sower

People gathered from far and wide to listen to Jesus

2. SERMON ON THE MOUNT

The Sermon on the Mount is the most famous of all Jesus' sermons. Which prayer does it include?

- Thanksgiving prayer
- the Lord's prayer
- the Mountain prayer

4. GOOD SAMARITAN

In the parable of the Good Samaritan, does the Samaritan:

- help an injured person
- build a hospital
- bring a leper to be healed by Jesus?

The Samaritan put wine and oil on the wound before wrapping it in bandages

At harvest time, crops were cut using a sickle

The prodigal son is welcomed home by his father

9. KINGDOM

Jesus often talked about a kingdom that was different from any other kingdom. Not a physical place, what is this kingdom called?

10. FOLLOWING JESUS

Jesus taught people not to love money, but to be "rich toward God". He compared a rich person following Him to a camel passing through the eye of – what?

7. PARABLE OF THE WEEDS

In this parable, a man sows wheat in a field, and his enemy sows weeds. The man represents God. Who does his enemy represent?

Camels appear in many Bible stories

6. PRODIGAL SON

In the parable of the prodigal son, does the prodigal son:

- kill his brother
- waste his money
- follow Jesus?

8. SINNER

Jesus was criticized for making friends with "sinners." What did Zacchaeus, a tax collector, do when Jesus befriended him?

- heal the sick
- betray Jesus
- give his money away

11. TALENTS

In the parable of the talents, does Jesus tell us that it is better to use the talents we have, or to save them?

Zacchaeus climbed a tree in order to see Jesus

Talents were not coins. They represented a large weight, or a lot of money

Death and resurrection

The crowd cheered Jesus and spread palm leaves on the road before Him

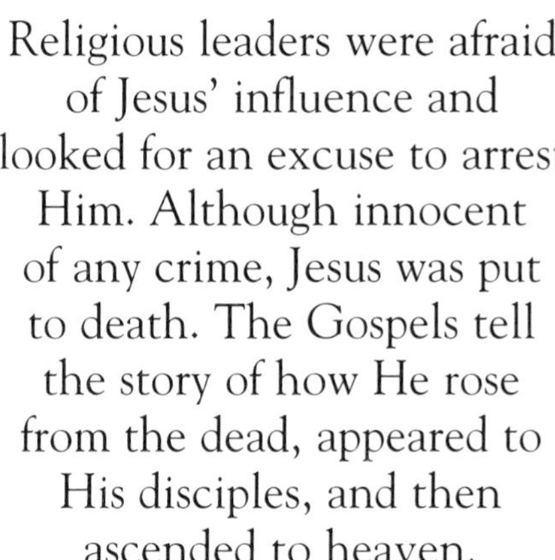

Religious leaders were afraid of Jesus' influence and looked for an excuse to arrest Him. Although innocent of any crime, Jesus was put to death. The Gospels tell the story of how He rose from the dead, appeared to His disciples, and then ascended to heaven.

The city of Jerusalem is important in several world religions

1. JERUSALEM

When Jesus entered Jerusalem for the last time, what did He ride?

- a donkey
- a horse
- a camel

Jesus threw the traders out of the Temple in Jerusalem, saying it should be a "house of prayer"

2. BETRAYAL

What did Judas get for betraying Jesus?

- thirty pieces of silver
- twenty pieces of gold
- two goats

Judas Iscariot was one of Jesus' closest disciples, but he betrayed Him

Jesus and His disciples at the Last Supper

3. LAST SUPPER

Who washed everybody's feet before the Last Supper?

- Peter
- James
- Jesus

4. ARRESTED

Soldiers came to arrest Jesus. Where did they find Him?

- in the Temple
- in the streets of Jerusalem
- in the Garden of Gethsemane

In Jesus' time, it was customary for people to have the dust washed from their feet when entering a house

Jesus blessed the bread and wine at the Last Supper

5. ROMAN LEADER

Who ordered Jesus' execution knowing that He was innocent?

- Julius Caesar
- Pontius Pilate
- Nero

6. RISING FROM DEAD

On which day of the week did Jesus rise from the dead?

Jesus was laid in a tomb cut out of rock

7. CEREMONY

At the Last Supper, Jesus blessed the bread and wine and told His disciples these represented His body and blood. Which Christian ceremony celebrates this?

- Baptism
- Communion
- Ordination

Jesus was nailed to a cross and left to die. The cross, or crucifix, is a Christian symbol

One Apostle had to touch Jesus' wounds before he would believe Jesus had risen from the dead

8. DOUBT

Which Apostle refused to believe that Jesus had risen from the dead until he could touch Him?

- Bartholomew
- Andrew
- Thomas

9. FESTIVAL

At which festival do Christians remember Jesus' death and resurrection?

10. SALVATION

According to the Apostles' teaching, Jesus died to save people from:

- their taxes
- themselves
- their sins?

Jesus told one of His disciples, "Before the rooster crows twice, you will disown me three times"

11. DENIAL

Which one of Jesus' disciples denied Him three times on the night of His arrest and trial?

- Matthew
- John
- Peter

12. ASCENSION

Jesus ascended to heaven forty days after He rose from the dead. Who witnessed this?

Angels appeared at the Ascension proclaiming that Jesus would return

The early Church

After Jesus ascended to heaven, His Apostles led the early Christians and taught others about Christ. The Christian community, called the "Church," grew rapidly, in spite of suffering much persecution. From the first community in Jerusalem, Christianity spread across the Roman Empire and beyond.

The dove is often used as a symbol in Christianity

1. HOLY TRINITY

In the New Testament, God is Father, Son, and Holy Spirit, yet still one God. Which of the three is sometimes represented by a dove?

- Father
- Son
- Holy Spirit

As they went to the Temple to pray, Peter and John met a beggar who had been unable to walk from birth

Many early Christians were put to death because of their beliefs

4. MARTYR

People who are killed because of what they believe are called martyrs. Who was the first Christian martyr?

- James
- Stephen
- John

Peter was imprisoned by enemies of the Church, but an angel appeared and released him from his chains

2. MIRACLES

When Peter and John met a beggar at the gate of the Temple, what did Peter tell the beggar to do?

- give them his money
- rise up and walk
- join their church

3. HOLY SPIRIT

After Jesus' death, His disciples gathered in Jerusalem. Fifty days later, they were "filled with the Holy Spirit." At which feast did this happen?

- Passover
- Pentecost
- Halloween

Paul had to escape from Damascus

5. ROAD TO DAMASCUS

Who began to believe in Christ after he was blinded by a heavenly light?

- Pontius Pilate
- Paul
- Titus

9. THE CHURCH

In the New Testament, what is the Church called?

- the spirit of Christ
- the sword of Christ
- the body of Christ

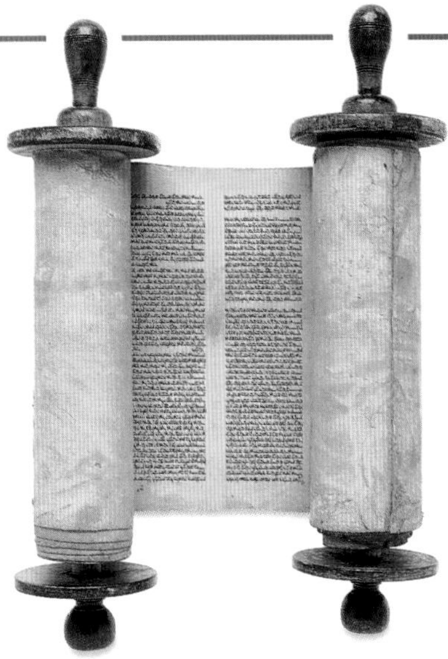

The Bible was originally recorded on scrolls

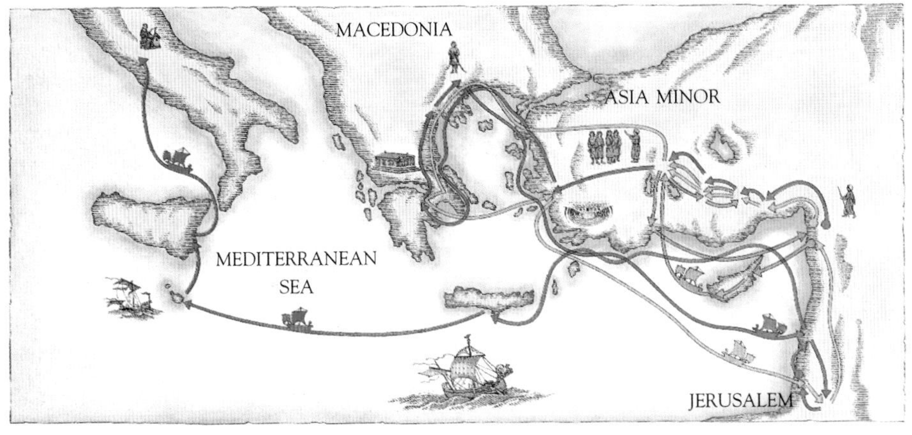

Paul traveled far and wide to preach about the life of Jesus

10. LETTERS

In his first letter to the Corinthians, Paul taught them about three important Christian beliefs. Which did he say was the greatest?

- faith
- hope
- love

6. FAMOUS SAYING

Which of these sayings is in the New Testament?

- love is God
- God is love
- all is God

7. VISIONS

Which New Testament book contains spectacular visions of God, heaven, and the end of history?

- Acts
- Revelation
- Romans

Of the 27 books of the New Testament, 21 are letters, known as "epistles"

8. THE ROCK

Which of the following Apostles was named the "Rock" by Jesus and made the leader of the Apostles?

- Peter
- Paul
- John

Paul is named as the author of 13 of the 21 New Testament letters

Answers

The Holy Book

1. THE BIBLE
Books. The word Bible comes from the Greek word "byblia," meaning books.

2. ONE GOD
Jerusalem. It was destroyed in AD 70. Only one wall remains – the Western Wall.

3. GLOBAL BOOK
349. Another 841 languages have the complete New Testament, and another 933 have at least one book of the Bible.

4. NEW LANGUAGE
Greek. At the time the New Testament was written, Greek was spoken across much of the Mediterranean and the Middle East.

5. ANIMALS
The sheep. Sheep are mentioned 200 times, and lambs 188 times.

6. LEADER
The servant of all. Jesus said that He had not come "to be served, but to serve, and to give His life as a ransom for many."

7. BIBLE SETTING
Canaan. It lies at the crossroads between Africa, Asia, and Europe.

8. THE LAW
The Torah. Torah means "teaching" and "guidance" as well as "law."

9. OLDEST SCROLLS
By the Dead Sea, at a place called Qumran. They are called the Dead Sea Scrolls.

10. BIBLE WRITERS
More than 30, over many centuries.

11. PRINT
1455. It was printed in Germany by Johannes Gutenburg.

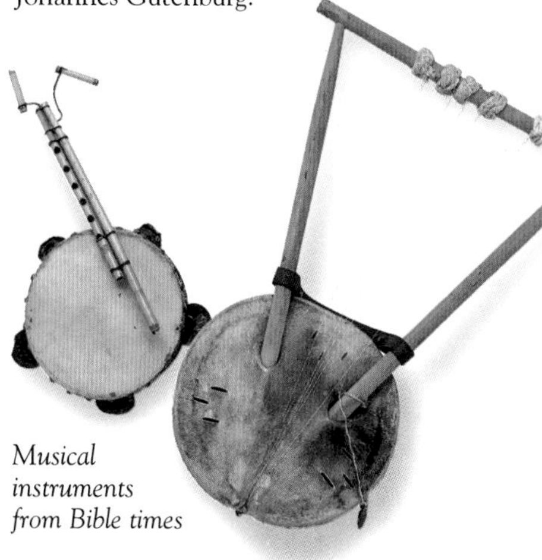

Musical instruments from Bible times

12. BIBLE DIVISIONS
Wisdom books. They are beautiful poems, written to be sung when worshiping God.

In the beginning

1. SIX DAYS
Day and night. The sun and moon were not created until the fourth day.

2. MURDER
Cain. He was jealous of his brother Abel.

3. GREAT FLOOD
Noah, a righteous (good) man.

4. THE TOWER
Babylon. God was displeased with the tower the residents of Babel built, so He confused their language and scattered them across the world.

Stained glass window depicting the Ascension

5. PARADISE
A garden. God created the Garden of Eden where life was perfect.

6. SIGN FROM GOD
A rainbow. The rainbow was a sign of hope, promising that God would never send such a flood on the earth again.

7. ABRAHAM'S JOURNEYS
Modern-day Iraq. Abraham was born in the city of Ur

8. ANCIENT ANCESTRY
The Jews and the Arabs. In Islam, Abraham is called Ibrahim, and is seen as the first true worshiper of God.

9. GREATEST SACRIFICE
Isaac. In the end God asked Abraham to sacrfice a ram (male sheep), and not Isaac (Genesis 22:1-19).

10. INHERITANCE
Esau. He was Isaac's eldest son, but he gave up his inheritance rights to his younger brother when he was hungry one day.

11. NEW NAME
Israel, which means "he struggles with God" (Genesis 32:22-32).

12. PILLAR OF SALT
Sodom. Gomorrah was a neighboring city, equally infamous, that was destroyed at the same time (Genesis 19:12-29).

13. OLD AGE
Methuselah. He is said to have lived to be 969 years old (Genesis 5:27).

The Israelites in Egypt

1. FAVORITE SON
Twelve. The twelve tribes of Israel descended from these twelve sons.

2. JOSEPH'S DREAM
Bow down to his sheaf. The dream foretold the time when he would be the king of Egypt's second-in-command.

3. SLAVERY
Pharaoh, which was the title of the ancient Egyptian kings.

4. BIRTH OF MOSES
In the river. His mother had hidden him because the king had said that all Israelite baby boys should be killed.

5. GOD'S PLAGUES
Ten: plagues of blood, frogs, gnats, flies, a plague on livestock, plagues of boils, hail, locusts, darkness, and the death of the Egyptians' first-born sons (Exodus 7:11).

6. PUNISHMENT
Bricks without straw. Straw was a vital part of the brick-making process.

7. EGYPTIAN RELIGION
Many gods. The chief god was the sun god.

8. TRIBES OF ISRAEL
Levi, the tribe to which Moses belonged.

9. TO THE PROMISED LAND
Milk and honey.

10. BURNING BUSH
God. Moses was told that God was going to rescue the Israelites and lead them out of Egypt (Exodus 3).

11. PRINT
1455. It was printed in Germany by Johannes Gutenberg.

The gate to the city of Jerusalem

The Exodus

1. FREEDOM
The Passover meal. The last plague that God sent on Egypt was to kill all the Egyptians' first-born sons, but he "passed over" the Israelites and did not harm them.

2. TEN COMMANDMENTS
On Mount Sinai (Exodus 19–20:21). The Ten Commandments teach how to behave towards God and other people.

3. WILDERNESS
A pillar of fire (Exodus 13:21-22).

4. FALSE IDOL
A calf. Moses was furious when he found his people worshiping a false idol.

5. FORTY YEARS
Like wafers. The Israelites were sent this food by God.

6. TALKING DONKEY
Balaam. The story is told in the Book of Numbers.

7. WILDERNESS FOOD
Quail (Numbers 11:4–33).

8. TRUMPETS
The walls fell down.

9. LEADERS
Judges and other leaders, as recorded in the Book of Judges.

Storage jar from Bible times

10. MOSES
No. Moses died before they reached the Promised Land, but God allowed him to see it. Joshua led them into the Land.

11. ARK OF THE COVENANT
The two tablets on which the Ten Commandments were written.

Prophets and kings

1. STRONG MAN
His hair. When Delilah found this out, she told Samson's enemies, the Philistines. They cut it and his strength left him.

2. HOLY MAN
Saul. He was a young man from the least important family of the smallest of the twelve tribes of Israel.

3. GIANT SLAYER
David. He succeeded Saul as king of Israel. David also wrote many of the psalms.

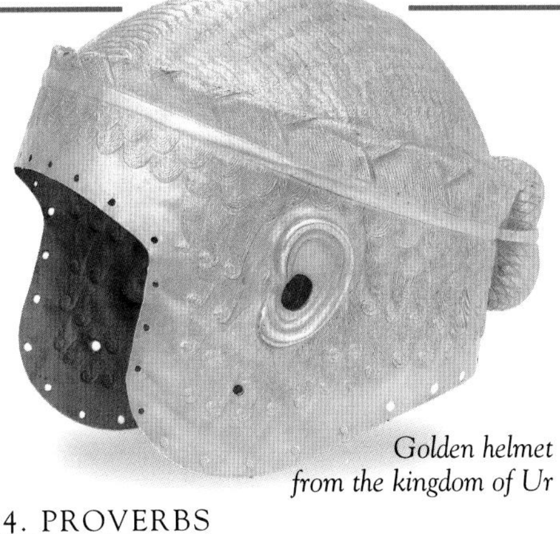

Golden helmet from the kingdom of Ur

4. PROVERBS
A cheerful look brings joy to the heart. There is a whole book in the Bible called Proverbs.

5. BEARING GIFTS
The queen of Sheba. She visited Solomon because she had heard of his great wisdom.

6. WISE LEADER
King Solomon. He was the richest and most powerful king of Israel.

7. PROPHET IN THE WILDERNESS
Brought him food (1 Kings 17:1-6). Elijah was a great prophet.

8. EXILE
70 years. Cyrus, a king of Persia, conquered Babylon and allowed the Israelites to go home (Ezra 1:1-4).

9. SAVING HER PEOPLE
Esther. The story of how she saved her people is recorded in the Book of Esther.

10. WRITING
Belshazzar. A disembodied hand appeared and wrote his fate on a wall (Daniel 5).

11. PROPHECY
Isaiah (Isaiah 53). Christians take this to be a prophecy of the coming of Jesus.

12. FISHY TALE
Jonah. He eventually went to Nineveh and saved the city from sin.

13. FAITH IN GOD
Because Daniel disobeyed Darius. A ruling was issued saying that people must only worship the king. Any man who disobeyed would be thrown to the lions.

The birth of Jesus

1. HOLY BIRTHPLACE
Bethlehem. There was an ancient prophecy that the Messiah would be born in Bethlehem.

2. MARY AND JOSEPH
Joseph is traditionally said to have been a carpenter. Jesus is believed to have worked as a carpenter as he grew up.

3. PREPARING THE WAY
John, known as John the Baptist (Luke 1:5-80). He was a preacher and baptized Jesus before He started His ministry.

4. GOD WITH US
Emmanuel (Matthew 1:23). This reflects the Biblical belief that Jesus was the Son of God. Christ and Messiah both mean "Annointed One": "Christ" is Greek, "Messiah" is Hebrew.

5. ANNUNCIATION
An angel named Gabriel (Luke 1:26-38).

6. RULERS
The Romans. There was also a king named Herod, who had been appointed by the Romans and was under their control.

7. FIRST TO HEAR
Some local shepherds. An angel appeared to them and said, "Today...a savior has been born to you; He is Christ the Lord."

8. PRECIOUS GIFTS
Wise men. They came from the East, guided by a star (Matthew 2:1-12).

9. ANGELS
"Messenger." Angels are God's messengers.

10. FLEEING HEROD
Egypt. Herod thought that Jesus was a threat to him because the wise men had said that Jesus was born King of the Jews.

Stories and miracles

1. DESERT DIET
John the Baptist, the prophet who heralded Jesus' arrival.

2. BAPTISM
In the Jordan River. When Jesus was baptized, a voice spoke from heaven, saying "You are my Son, whom I love; with you I am well pleased" (Luke 3:21-22).

3. THE GOSPELS
Four – named Matthew, Mark, Luke, and John. Each focuses on a different aspect of Jesus' ministry.

4. DISCIPLES
"Fishers of men," who would call others to follow Jesus.

A desert meal

5. MINISTRY
The Good Shepherd (John 10:1-21), who "lays down his life for the sheep" – as Jesus was to lay down His life on the Cross.

6. TEMPTATION
The devil. Jesus was tempted for forty days. He resisted His temptation by quoting the Old Testament.

7. GOSPEL SAYINGS
It is more blessed to give than to receive. It is recorded in the Book of Acts.

8. HONEST QUESTION
A rich, young ruler. He asked how he could be perfect, and Jesus told him to give away all he had and to follow Him.

9. RELIGIOUS LEADERS
The Pharisees. They followed religious laws very strictly. When they objected to Jesus breaking the Sabbath laws, Jesus said, "The Sabbath was made for man, not man for the Sabbath" (Mark 2:27).

10. FEAST
5,000 (Luke 9:10-17).

11. FRIENDS
Lazarus (John 11:1-45).

12. WATER INTO WINE
At a wedding, at Cana in Galilee (John 2:1-11). He turned water into wine.

13. TRANSFIGURATION
Moses and Elijah (Mark 9:2-13).

Teaching and traveling

1. DISCIPLES
Apostles. The word "apostle" comes from one of the Greek words for messenger.

2. SERMON ON THE MOUNT
The Lord's Prayer. The Sermon on the Mount is recorded in Matthew.

3. WRITTEN RECORD
No. As far as is known Jesus left all the recordings of His life and teaching to His followers.

4. GOOD SAMARITAN
Help an injured person. Jesus told this parable to answer the question "Who is my neighbor?", showing that it is possible to be a neighbor to anyone in need (Luke 10:25-37).

Jug for storing wine

5. WORD OF GOD
Parable of the sower. The different types of ground illustrate different responses to hearing the Word of God.

6. PRODIGAL SON
He wastes all the money his father has given him.

7. PARABLE OF THE WEEDS
The devil (Matthew 13:24-43).

8. SINNER
He gave away his money. Tax collectors were hated because they worked for the Romans and were often corrupt.

9. KINGDOM
The kingdom of God, or the kingdom of heaven.

10. FOLLOWING JESUS
A needle. Jesus said that this was possible with God's help (Luke 12:21).

Stained glass window depicting St Stephen, the first Christian martyr

11. TALENTS
To use them (Matthew 25:14–30).

Death and resurrection

1. JERUSALEM
A donkey, to fulfill an Old Testament prophecy.

2. BETRAYAL
Thirty pieces of silver. After betraying Jesus he was overcome with guilt and hanged himself.

3. LAST SUPPER
Jesus, to remind his apostles to be humble and to serve others.

4. ARRESTED
The Garden of Gethsemane. Jesus had gone there to pray.

5. ROMAN LEADER
Pontius Pilate, the Roman governor of Palestine.

6. RISING FROM DEAD
Sunday, which is why His followers made Sunday their day of rest.

7. CEREMONY
Communion. Christians remember Jesus' death on the cross at Communion.

8. DOUBT
Thomas. This is why he is often referred to as "Doubting Thomas."

9. FESTIVAL
Easter – the Last Supper and Jesus' arrest on Maundy Thursday, His death on Good Friday, and His resurrection on Easter Sunday.

10. SALVATION
From their sins (the wrong in them that keeps them far from God).

11. DENIAL
Peter (Mark 14:66-72).

12. ASCENSION
Several of the disciples, including Peter, Thomas, James, and John.

The early Church

1. HOLY TRINITY
The Holy Spirit. When Jesus was baptized by John the Baptist, the Holy Spirit appeared in the form of a dove.

2. MIRACLES
Rise up and walk (Acts 3:1-10).

3. HOLY SPIRIT
Pentecost – a festival celebrating the first fruits of the harvest.

4. MARTYR
Stephen. He was a leader in the first church in Jerusalem.

5. ROAD TO DAMASCUS
Paul. A "light from heaven" shone down on him and Jesus spoke to him from the light (Acts 9:1-19).

6. FAMOUS SAYING
God is love (1 John 4:16).

7. VISIONS
Revelation. Acts deals with the acts of the apostles, and Romans is a letter to the church at Rome.

8. THE ROCK
Peter. Peter means "rock," his original name was Simon.

9. THE CHURCH
The body of Christ.

10. LETTERS
Love (1 Corinthians 13:1-13).

Fishes and loaves

Index

A B C

D E F

G H I

J K L

M N O P

R S T

U W Z

Acknowledgments

DK would like to thank:
Sarah Ponder for designing the symbols. Iain Morris and Carlton Hibbert for design assistance. Miranda Smith for proof-reading. Marion Dent for the index.

Additional photography:
Ashmolean Museum, British Library, British Museum, Peter Chadwick, Andy Crawford, Geoff Dann, Glasgow Museums, Christi Graham and Nick Nicholls, Frank Greenaway, Peter Hayman, Alan Hills, Barnabus Kindersley, Dave King, Cyril Laubscher, Museum of London, Lawrence Pordes, St. Mungo's Museum

Picture credits:
(t=top b=bottom c=center l=left r=right)
The publisher woould like to thank the following for their kind permission to reproduce the photographs:
Ancient Art and Architecture Collection: / B. Norman 4tc; / Ronald Sheridan 12br; 16tl; 22bc; 28t
Bridgeman Art Library, London: / British Library London 16tr; / Giraudon 23cr; / Index 23 br; / Kunsthistorisches Museum, Vienna 8br
Sonia Halliday & Laura Lushington: 4 bc; 6c; 14tr; 24tr; 26t
The Calling of the Apostles Peter and Andrew, Duccio di Buoninsegna, **Samuel H. Kress Collection © 1996 Board of Trustees, National Gallery of Art, Washington:** 18bl
Tony Stone Images: / Sylvain Grandadam 22ar; / Sarah Stone 26br
Zefa Pictures: 6br
Every effort has been made to trace copyright holders of photographs and we apologize if any omissions have been made.